STRING ART

W9-CEM-900

KLUTZ.

SUPER-STYLISH STRING ART

You start with string, pins, paper, and a board. You end with adorable art. This book takes the mystery out of what happens in between.

Read The Basics and make the heart to learn the steps you need to do for every project. Use whatever background paper and string colors you like to give your string art a style that's all your own.

What you get

This book comes with just about everything you need to make six beautiful string art projects.

String

Ball-head pins

Easy-to-trace patterns

Pin-pushing tool

Only-from-Klutz tool to help you push in the pins just right

Pins

Background paper

Tracing paper

Project boards

Want to make more?

Check out Klutz.com for extra supplies, or visit your local craft or fabric store.

Thin paper, like origami or wrapping paper, tends to works best for the background paper. The string is also called craft thread or cord. For pins, look for size 14 (22 mm) beading pins. To make a backing board, glue together three layers of corrugated cardboard.

YOU'LL ALSO NEED
- tape
- pencil or fine-tip marker
- scissors
- glue

the Basics

Please read this section before you start. It explains steps you'll do for every project: Trace the pattern • Wrap the board • Insert the pins • Tie on and tie off

Trace the Pattern

1 Flip through the book and pick a project you want to make. Then find the matching pattern in the back of the book.

Start with a pattern and end with beautiful art. The instructions for this heart are on page 15.

SCRIBBLE

Heart

Whale

2 Line up a sheet of tracing paper that matches the size of your design (big or small) with the corners framing the pattern. Do not tear out the page.

3 Trace the pattern's dots, which show where you will insert the pins. Then set aside the tracing paper.

Tip: You can trace the pattern with a pencil or a fine-tip marker.

Wrap the Board

This wrapping technique is different from the way most people wrap presents. It's a neat and tidy way to wrap a flat object.

1 Pick a sheet of background paper and a board that match the size of your project (big or small).

2 Lay the background paper on a flat surface with the front facing down. Center the board, lining it up with the rectangle printed on the back.

This side will show behind the pins and string.

3 Fold the paper over one long side of the board and tape. Then fold over the other side, pull the paper snug, and tape.

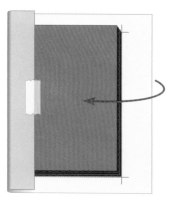

4 At one end, push both sides of the paper in. Crease the paper to create a flat bottom flap.

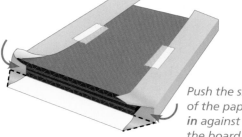

*Push the sides of the paper **in** against the board.*

5 Crease the paper to create a flat top flap.

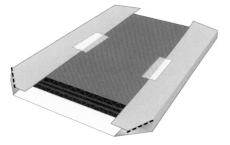

Similar colors, like blue and green, are calm and cool.

Bright colors stand out against a light background, letting the string be the star.

To reverse a pattern, flip over the tracing paper with the pattern drawn on it before you insert the pins.

PICK A BACKGROUND

When you choose background paper, imagine what your string design will look like on it.

6 Fold the top flap down over the edge of the board. Flatten and crease it along the bottom edge of the board.

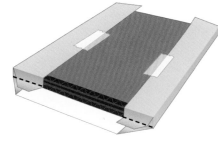

7 Fold the bottom flap up and tape it tightly on each side.

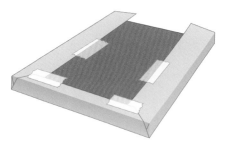

8 Repeat steps 4–7 on the other end.

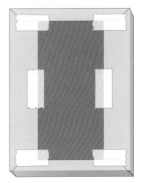

HOW TO USE THE TOOL

Using the pin-pushing tool to insert pins makes it easy on your fingers and helps keep the pins the same height.

1 Hold a pin steady and upright and poke its point through a dot on the tracing paper into the board, just enough so it won't fall out.

Before you insert a pin all the way, make sure it's standing straight up and down. If it's leaning, pull it out and try again.

You can also use the indentation on the tool to push the pin in partway.

Tip: If a pin becomes loose in a hole, take it out and insert it into a new hole nearby.

You want pins to be straight like this...   *...not like this.*

2 When the pin is straight, use the tool to push it in all the way.

Hold the pin steady and upright, put the pin-pushing tool over it...

...and press straight down until the tool touches the surface. Lift the tool off and go on to the next pin.

3 After you insert all the pins, check that they are all the same height. If they are, the tops will line up. If some tops are higher than others, use the pin-pushing tool to push the pins in all the way.

You want pins to be even like this...   *...not like this.*

Insert the Pins

The tracing paper lets you place the pins right where you need them.

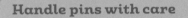

These are used for stringing.

Use these not these

These are used as accents.

1 Lay the tracing paper with the design on it on the front of the wrapped board. Line up the paper and board edges.

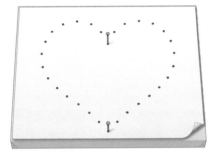

To hold the tracing paper in place, use the pin-pushing tool to insert pins through one dot at the top and one at the bottom of the pattern.

2 Insert a pin in each dot until they're all pinned.

3 When every dot has a pin inserted in it, carefully tear off the tracing paper.

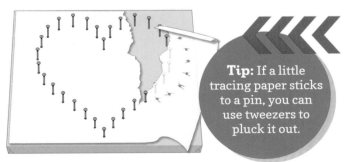

Tip: If a little tracing paper sticks to a pin, you can use tweezers to pluck it out.

Handle pins with care

- Work on a flat surface when inserting pins. Don't hold the board in your lap or hands.

- If a pin gets stuck in the pin-pushing tool, ask an adult to help get it out.

- Throw out any bent pin and use a new one.

- If a pin pokes out the back of the board, pull the pinhead up from the front until the pin no longer pokes out.

- Put pins away when you're not using them and keep them away from kids under ten.

- If a pin poke does break the skin, wash and bandage the area.

Tie On and Tie Off

You **tie on** the string to the pin where you want to start a color. When you end a color, you **tie off** the string.

START A COLOR (Tie On)

Often it doesn't matter where you tie on. If you need to tie on to a specific pin, the instructions will tell you.

1 Loop one end of the string around the pin. Tie a half-knot (see below) and pull it tight.

— *Leave a tail of about 4 inches (10 cm) long.*

2 Tie another half-knot on top of the first one and pull it tight.

3 Cut off the string, taking care not to cut too close to the knot.

Leave a tail about ⅛ inch (.3 cm) long

4 Apply a dot of glue to the knot. This will help keep the knot secure and prevent fraying.

HOW TO WORK WITH STRING

Pull gently on the string to keep it from coming off the pins. You want to pull the string snug — not too loose and not too tight.

If the string does come off the pins, don't panic. Just re-loop it around the pins and keep going.

If you don't like how your project is looking, unwrap the string from the pins and start again.

You want the string to look like this...

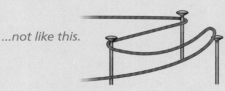

Tip: To help control the string, pinch it and work close to the pins. Let the string slide through your fingers as needed.

...not like this.

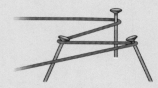

Too loose. *String that's not snug enough can slide off the pins.*

Too tight. *String that's too snug can make the pins lean — and possibly pop out.*

END A COLOR (Tie Off)

Tying off is the trickiest part of string art. It often takes practice and sometimes an extra set of hands to get the hang of it, but don't worry, you will.

Tip: If you need help tying off and no one is around, tape the tail of the string to the back of the board to hold it tight.

1 Loop the string around the last pin a couple of times, pull it snug, and cut it.

Leave a tail of about 4 inches (10 cm) long.

2 With one hand, hold the string snug close to the pin. With the other hand, tie a half-knot close to the pin.

To tie a half-knot, loop the loose end of the string around the string that you're holding snug.

3 Drop the half-knot over the pin and pull it tight. Do it again so you have two knots.

4 Cut the string and put a dot of glue on the knot, the same way you did when you tied on.

SCRIBBLE

"Scribbling" with string is like scribbling with a marker. The best part: Pretty much anything goes. Really. Go up and down. Side to side. Diagonally. Scribbling is a great way to fill in shapes.

WHAT YOU NEED

- 1 small board
- 1 small background paper
- heart pattern (page 47)
- 1 small tracing paper
- 30 pins
- pin-pushing tool
- 1 color of string

YOU'LL ALSO NEED
- tape
- pencil or fine-tip marker
- scissors
- glue

Heart

This first project gives you a chance to get the hang of working with the string so that it's not too loose and not too tight, but just right.

1 Follow the instructions on pages 6–11 to trace the heart pattern, wrap the board, and insert the pins. Tear off the tracing paper.

2 Tie on the string to any pin. (See page 12.)

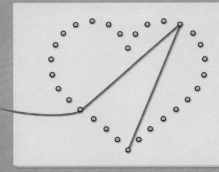

3 Loop the string around another pin to change its direction...

The string makes a U-turn around the pin.

Instructions continue on next page ⟫⟫⟫

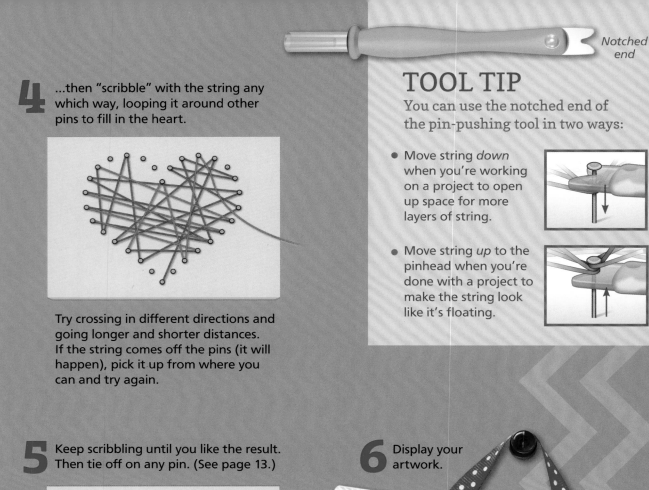

4 ...then "scribble" with the string any which way, looping it around other pins to fill in the heart.

Try crossing in different directions and going longer and shorter distances. If the string comes off the pins (it will happen), pick it up from where you can and try again.

Notched end

TOOL TIP

You can use the notched end of the pin-pushing tool in two ways:

- Move string *down* when you're working on a project to open up space for more layers of string.

- Move string *up* to the pinhead when you're done with a project to make the string look like it's floating.

5 Keep scribbling until you like the result. Then tie off on any pin. (See page 13.)

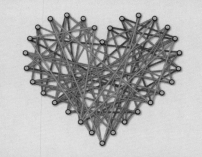

6 Display your artwork.

Tip: To hang your art, tape a loop of ribbon to the back.

Whether it's a **twinkling star**, a **sweet heart**, or **looping letters**, scribbling lets you fill in any shape in no time. You can create your own pattern by drawing a shape on tracing paper and marking dots where you want the pins. To shine bright, see page 46 for the **Scribble Star** pattern.

WHAT YOU NEED

- 1 small board
- 1 small background paper
- whale pattern (page 47)
- 1 small tracing paper
- 62 pins
- pin-pushing tool
- 2 colors of string
- 1 ball-head pin

YOU'LL ALSO NEED

- tape
- pencil or fine-tip marker
- scissors
- glue

Whale

1 Trace the whale pattern, wrap the board, and insert the pins. Tear off the tracing paper. Tie on the first color of string where shown.

2 Scribble to fill in the whale, avoiding the inside of the whale's mouth. When you like how it looks, tie off on any pin.

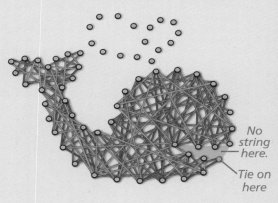

No string here.

Tie on here

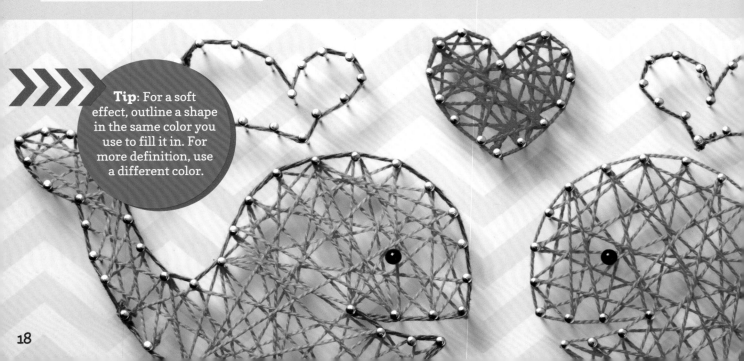

Tip: For a soft effect, outline a shape in the same color you use to fill it in. For more definition, use a different color.

3 Tie on the second color of string to a pin on the whale's body and outline it (see sidebar below). Tie off.

4 Tie on the second color of string to a pin on the spouted water and outline it. Tie off.

Tip: For a stronger outline, go around a shape multiple times.

5 Insert a ball-head pin for the eye where you think it looks good.

Tip: To avoid other areas when you scribble, you can outline what you're filling in with the same color before you scribble.

HOW TO OUTLINE

To outline a shape, start with the string at any outside pin, move to the pin next to it, and circle that pin with the string. Continue pin by pin until you finish the outline. To keep the line on the outside and consistent, circle the pins clockwise and circle the shape clockwise.

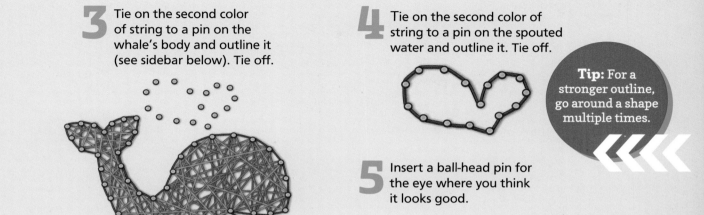

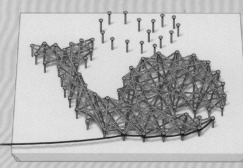

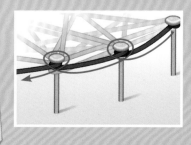

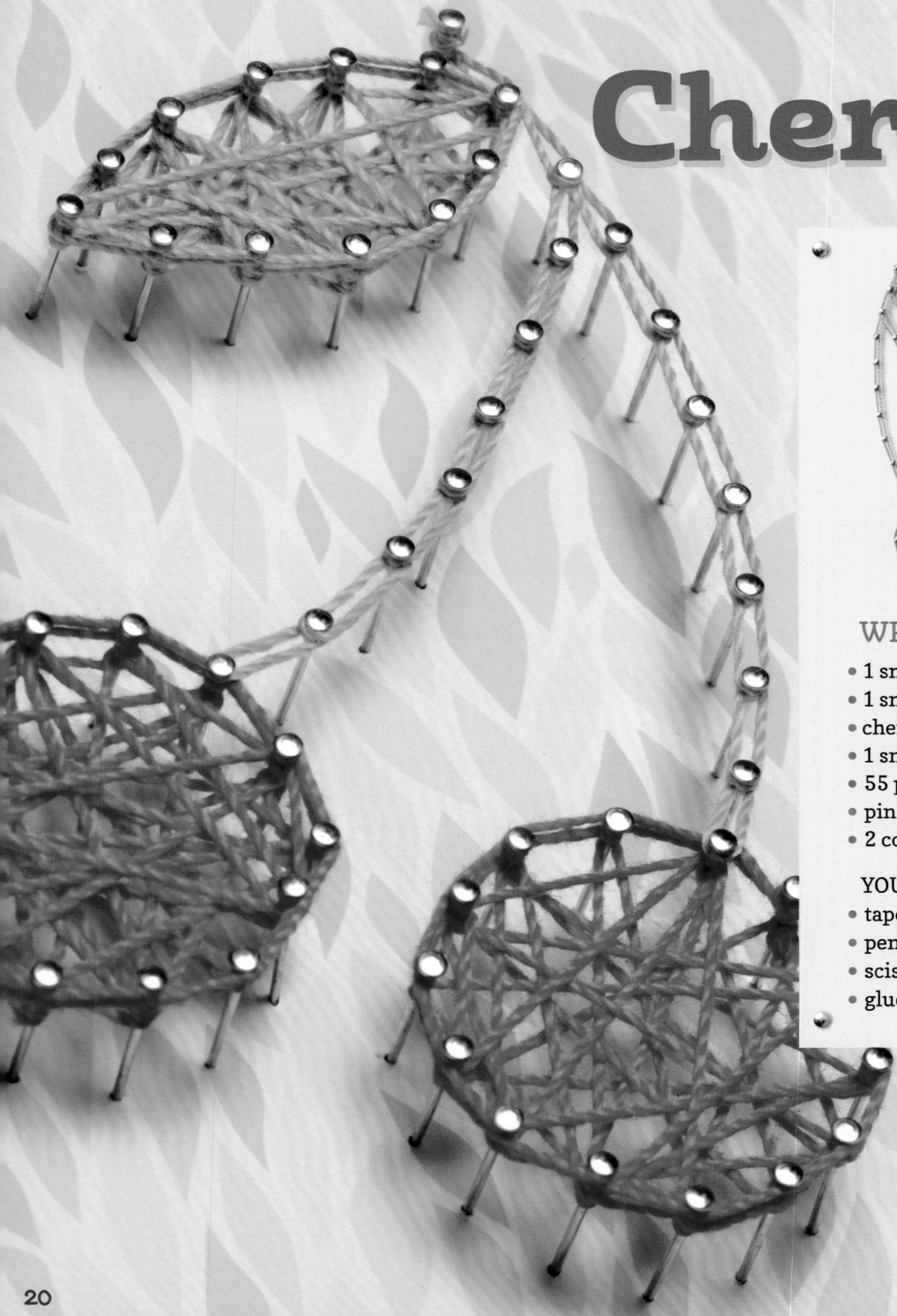

Cherries

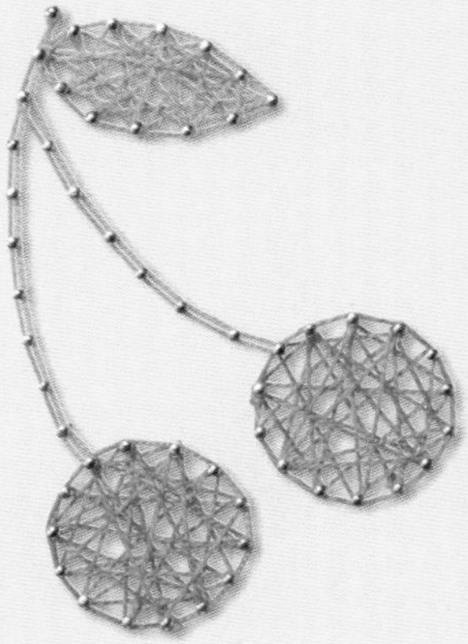

WHAT YOU NEED

- 1 small board
- 1 small background paper
- cherries pattern (page 48)
- 1 small tracing paper
- 55 pins
- pin-pushing tool
- 2 colors of string

YOU'LL ALSO NEED
- tape
- pencil or fine-tip marker
- scissors
- glue

1 Trace the cherries pattern, wrap the board, and insert the pins. Tear off the tracing paper.

2 Tie on the first color of string to one of the cherries on any pin. Scribble to fill in the cherry.

Without tying off, outline the cherry. For sharper edges go around the cherry 2–3 times. Tie off.

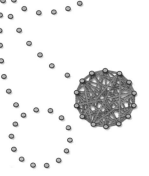

3 Repeat step 2 with the other cherry.

HOW TO DOUBLE OUTLINE

Outline as usual (see page 19), make a U-turn, and return to where you started, always looping clockwise.

As you outline each stem, you'll create a line moving toward a cherry. After you make a U-turn around the pin by the cherry, the line will fall on the other side of the pins, creating a double-line effect.

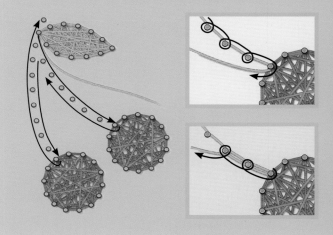

4 Tie on the second color of string to the leaf. Scribble to fill in the leaf.

Without tying off, outline the leaf, ending on the point of the leaf that touches the stem.

End here.

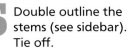

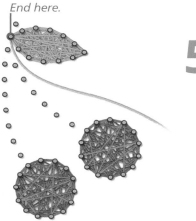

5 Double outline the stems (see sidebar). Tie off.

Locket

Where you don't put string can have as big an impact as where you do.

1 Trace the locket pattern, wrap the board, and insert the pins. Tear off the tracing paper.

2 Tie on anywhere and scribble to fill in the locket. Don't fill in the keyhole.

3 Outline the locket and the keyhole using the same color or a different color. Tie off.

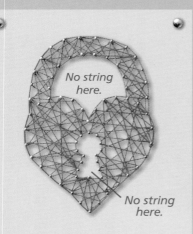

No string here.

No string here.

WHAT YOU NEED

- 1 small board
- 1 small background paper
- locket pattern (page 48)
- 1 small tracing paper
- 70 pins
- pin-pushing tool
- 1 or 2 colors of string

YOU'LL ALSO NEED
- tape
- pencil or fine-tip marker
- scissors
- glue

Mix it up: You can use a different color to fill in the handle or to outline.

Glasses

1 Trace the glasses pattern, wrap the board, and insert the pins except for the ball-head pins. Tear off the tracing paper.

2 Tie on anywhere and scribble to fill in the glasses.

3 Outline the glasses using the same color or a different color. Tie off.

4 Insert two ball-head pins at each outer corner of the frames.

When you're scribbling in a narrow space, as you are in these frames, go around the design once and then go over the same area again, filling it in more.

WHAT YOU NEED

- 1 large board
- 1 large background paper
- glasses pattern (page 49)
- 1 large tracing paper
- 85 pins
- pin-pushing tool
- 1 or 2 colors of string
- 4 ball-head pins

YOU'LL ALSO NEED
- tape
- pencil or fine-tip marker
- scissors
- glue

No string here

No string here

Love

Overlap different colors of string to fade from one color to the next. This creates an effect called **ombré** (pronounced "om-bray"), a French word that means "shading."

WHAT YOU NEED

- 1 large board
- 1 large background paper
- love pattern (page 50)
- 1 large tracing paper
- 116 pins
- pin-pushing tool
- 3 colors of string

YOU'LL ALSO NEED
- tape
- pencil or fine-tip marker
- scissors
- glue

1 Trace the love pattern, wrap the board, and insert the pins. Tear off the tracing paper.

2 Tie on the first color of string. Scribble and outline the first two letters, *L* and *O*. Tie off.

Mix it up: Instead of shading from one color to the next, you can use one color for all the letters or make each letter a different color.

3 Tie on the second color of string. Lightly scribble and outline the *right half* of the letter *O,* overlapping the first color. Then scribble and outline *all* of the letter *V*. Tie off.

Overlap the first color but also let it peek through, like one color is fading into the next.

4 Tie on the third color of string. Lightly scribble and outline the *right half* of the letter *V*, overlapping the second color. Then scribble and outline *all* of the letter *E*. Tie off.

FAN

Watch a lovely fan take shape as you loop string in and out, always returning to a center pin. Then group fans together into designs and see them attract fans all their own.

Butterfly

WHAT YOU NEED

- 1 small board
- 1 small background paper
- butterfly pattern (page 51)
- 1 small tracing paper
- 52 pins
- pin-pushing tool

YOU'LL ALSO NEED

- tape
- pencil or fine-tip marker
- scissors
- glue

1 Follow the instructions on pages 6–11 to trace the butterfly pattern, wrap the board, and insert the pins. Tear off the tracing paper.

2 Tie on the first color of string to the pin shown. (See page 12.)

3 Loop the string down around the pin directly below on the butterfly's left lower wing...

...then return to the first pin and loop around it.

Instructions continue on next page ⟫⟫⟫

4 Repeat step 3 moving pin by pin around the outside of the wing. Return to the center pin each time and loop around it.

Tip: Be extra careful not to pull too hard on the string. The center pin can easily pop out if the string is pulled too tight.

5 Finish filling in the left wing. Do not tie off.

6 Continuing with the same string, outline the left wing. Tie off. (See page 13.)

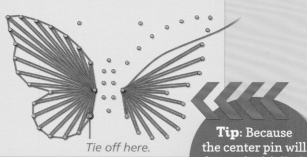

Tie off here.

Tie on, fan, and outline the right wing. Tie off.

Tip: Because the center pin will be stacked full of string, tie off on a different pin.

7 Using a different color of string, scribble the butterfly's body and outline each antenna.

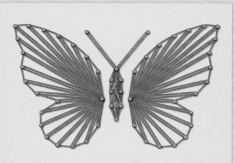

Enjoy a **burst of color** when you hang several pieces of string art together using ribbon on a bulletin board or wall. To display them on something metal, like a locker or refrigerator, use magnetic tape, sold at craft and office-supply stores.

Mix it up: Make the butterfly wings in two colors, then outline them in one of the colors.

Fan Star

Change things up with this clever star pattern, where fans go **in** — instead of **out** — to form a shape.

WHAT YOU NEED

- 1 small board
- 1 small background paper
- fan star pattern (page 51)
- 1 small tracing paper
- 26 pins
- pin-pushing tool
- 1 color of string

YOU'LL ALSO NEED
- tape
- pencil or fine-tip marker
- scissors
- glue

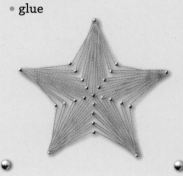

1 Trace the star pattern, wrap the board, and insert the pins. Tear off the tracing paper.

2 Tie on to an outer point of the star. Skip one pin and fan from left to right, in toward the center, seven times.

3 Continuing to the right, loop clockwise first around the next pin and then around the pin at the next outer point.

4 Repeat steps 2–3 until the star is filled in. Tie off.

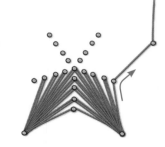

Flower

1 Trace the flower pattern, wrap the board, and insert the pins. Tear off the tracing paper.

2 Tie on the first color of string to the pin at the base of a petal. This will be the center pin of a fan.

Moving around the edge of the petal clockwise, skip the first pin and fan five times.

3 Starting with the left pin you skipped in step 1, outline the petal. Then outline from the base of this petal to the base of the next.

4 Repeat steps 2–3 until the petals are filled in. Tie off.

5 Tie on another color to the center pin and fan in a circle to fill in the flower's center. Outline the circle around the fan a few times. Tie off.

WHAT YOU NEED

- 1 small board
- 1 small background paper
- flower pattern (page 52)
- 1 small tracing paper
- 65 pins
- pin-pushing tool
- 2 colors of string

YOU'LL ALSO NEED

- tape
- pencil or fine-tip marker
- scissors
- glue

Fox

WHAT YOU NEED

- 1 small board
- 1 small background paper
- fox pattern (page 52)
- 1 small tracing paper
- 80 pins
- 2 ball-head pins
- pin-pushing tool
- 3 colors of string

YOU'LL ALSO NEED

- tape
- pencil or fine-tip marker
- scissors
- glue

1 Trace the fox pattern, wrap the board, and insert the pins, using the two ball-head pins for eyes. Tear off the tracing paper.

2 For the cheeks: Tie on the first color of string to one of the ball-head pins. Starting at the bottom inside pin as shown and moving away from the nose, fan ten times. Tie off. Repeat on the other side.

Tip: The right and left sides of the fox's face mirror each other, so the fans go in opposite directions.

3 For the outside of the ears: Tie on the same color of string to the pin in the ear as shown. Starting at the tip of the ear and going down the outside, fan six times. Repeat on the other side.

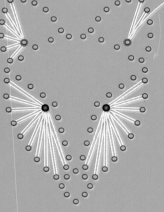

4 For the inside of the ears: Tie on the second color of string to the same pin you tied on to in step 3. Starting at the tip of the ear and overlapping the first color of string, fan six times. Tie off. Repeat on the other side.

5 Scribble and outline the forehead and snout in the second color.

6 Scribble and outline the nose in the third color.

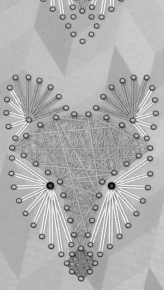

Dandelion

Wish upon this dandelion.
Add extra seeds for extra wishes.

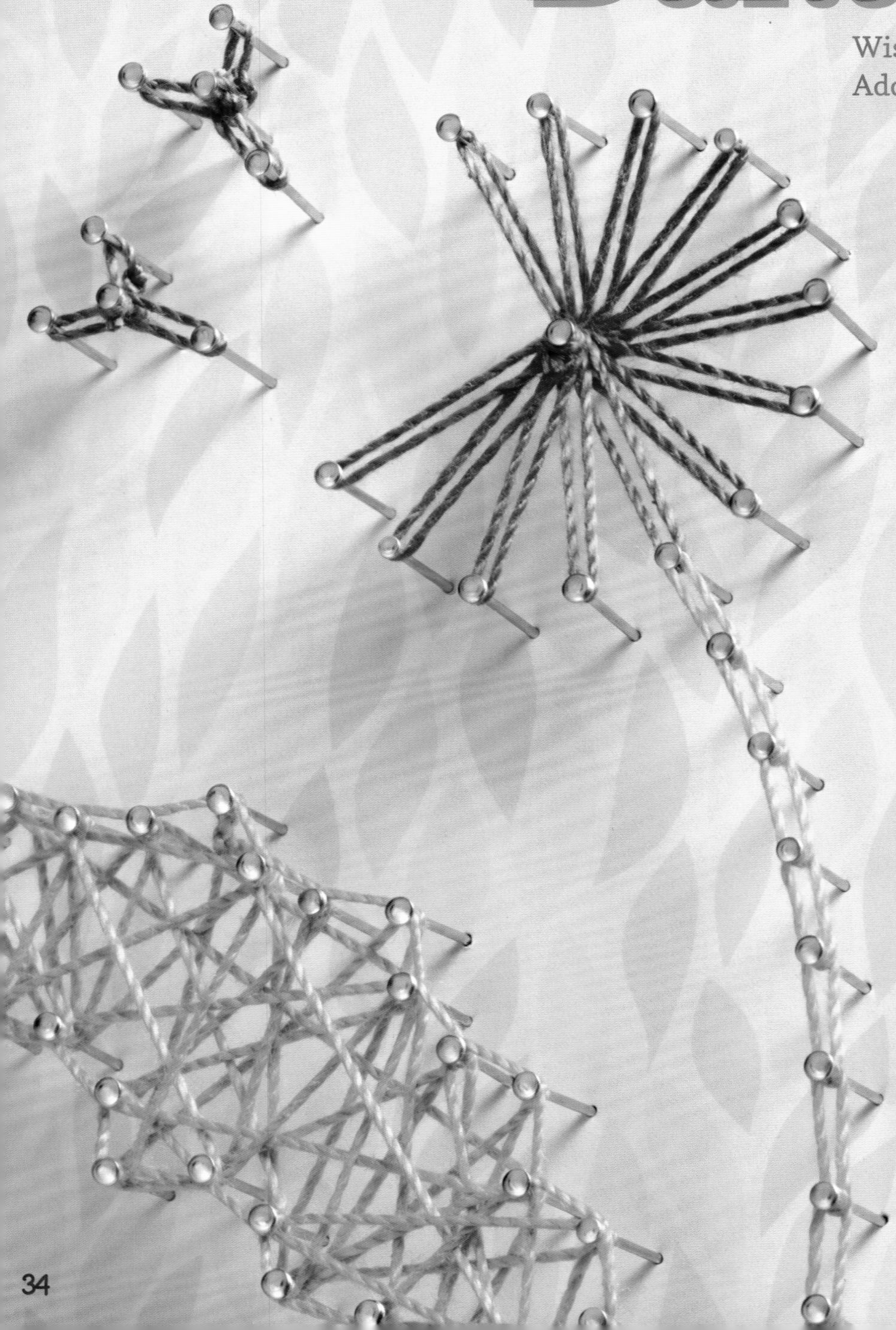

WHAT YOU NEED

- 1 small board
- 1 small background paper
- dandelion pattern (page 54)
- 1 small tracing paper
- 64 pins
- pin-pushing tool
- 2 colors of string

YOU'LL ALSO NEED

- tape
- pencil or fine-tip marker
- scissors
- glue

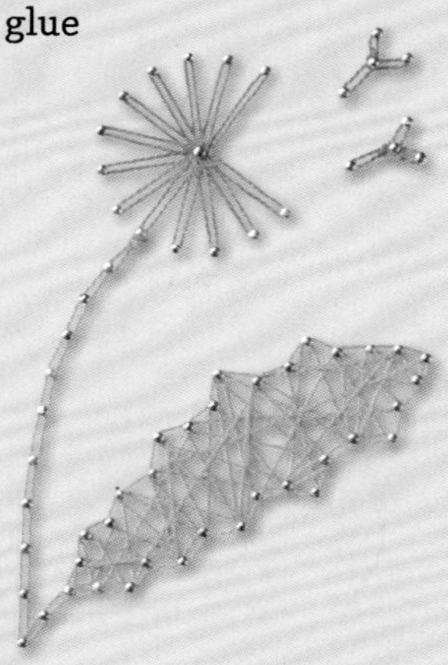

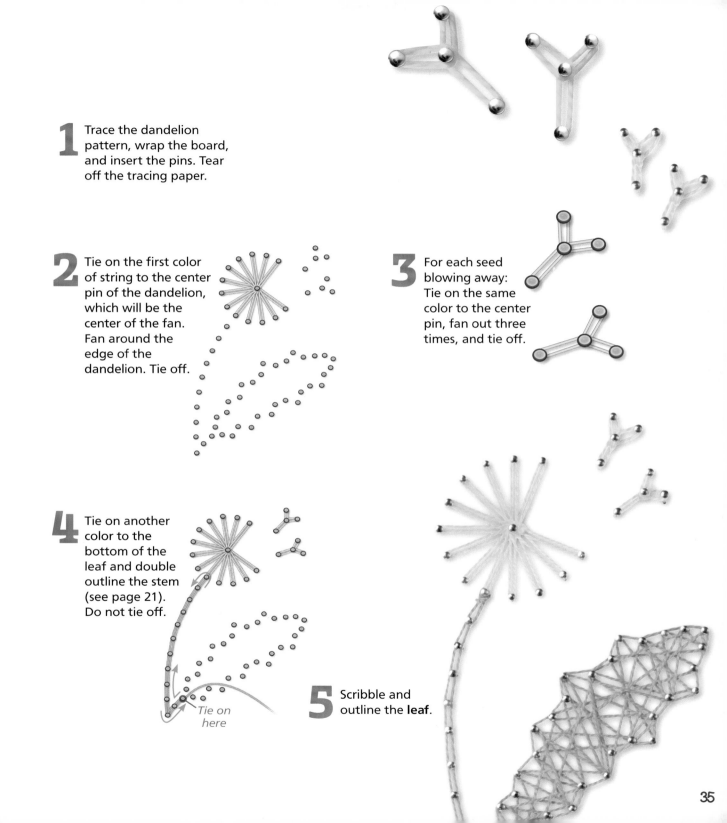

1 Trace the dandelion pattern, wrap the board, and insert the pins. Tear off the tracing paper.

2 Tie on the first color of string to the center pin of the dandelion, which will be the center of the fan. Fan around the edge of the dandelion. Tie off.

3 For each seed blowing away: Tie on the same color to the center pin, fan out three times, and tie off.

4 Tie on another color to the bottom of the leaf and double outline the stem (see page 21). Do not tie off.

Tie on here

5 Scribble and outline the **leaf**.

Owl

Now that you know how to fan, outline, and scribble, you're wise enough to take on this owl.

Before you start, make sure you have about 4 yards (3.7 m) of both the first and second colors of string.

WHAT YOU NEED

- 1 big board
- 1 large background paper
- owl pattern (page 53)
- 1 large tracing paper
- 102 pins
- 2 ball-head pins
- pin-pushing tool
- 3 colors of string

YOU'LL ALSO NEED

- tape
- pencil or fine-tip marker
- scissors
- glue

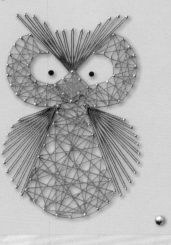

1 Trace the owl pattern, wrap the board, and insert the pins, using the two ball-head pins for the eyes. Tear off the tracing paper.

2 Tie on the first color of string to the top of one of the wings where shown. Starting at the top outer wing pin and moving down toward the center, fan ten times. Tie off where you tied on. Repeat on the other side.

3 Tie on the same color of string at the top of the beak where shown. Fan from the the top left pin to the top right pin. Tie off where you tied on.

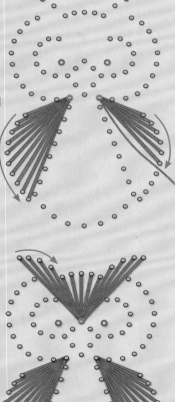

4 Using the second color of string, first outline then scribble the body and cheeks, avoiding the eye and beak areas.

— *No string here.*

Tip: To avoid other areas, outline the area you want to scribble first. For stronger edges, outline again after you scribble.

5 Using the third color of string, scribble the beak and outline it twice.

ZIGZAG

It makes sense that "zigzag" starts with Z. To zigzag, you weave string back and forth between two rows of pins, making a series of Zs along the way.

Feather

Zip this pretty feather together in no time, zigzagging down one side and up the other.

WHAT YOU NEED

- 1 small board
- 1 small background paper
- feather pattern (page 54)
- 1 small tracing paper
- 61 pins
- pin-pushing tool
- 2 colors of string

YOU'LL ALSO NEED

- tape
- pencil or fine-tip marker
- scissors
- glue

1 Follow the instructions on pages 6–11 to trace the feather pattern, wrap the board, and insert the pins. Tear off the tracing paper.

2 Tie on the first color of string to the top center pin. (See page 12.)

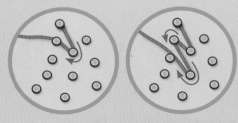

3 Start your zigzag by making a U-turn around the next pin in the center row.

Make a U-turn around the first pin in the row to the left, followed by a U-turn around the next pin in the center. You've just made a Z.

Instructions continue on next page ⟫⟫

4 Keep on making Zs between the left and center rows of pins until you reach the last pin on the left.

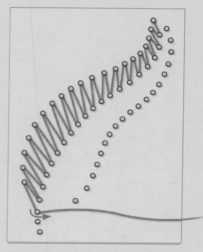

Change directions to head up the other side by wrapping the string around the third center pin from the bottom.

5 Zigzag between the right and center rows of pins until you reach the top pin, where you tied on. Tie off. (See page 13.)

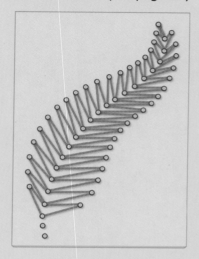

6 Tie on the second color of string to the bottom center pin. Double outline the center row (see page 21). Tie off. (See page 13.)

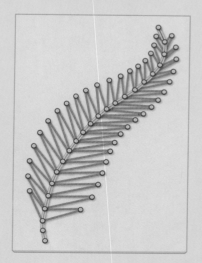

Tip: Sign your name or add your initials to your artwork.

A **picture frame** is like jewelry for art. It adds a finishing touch. A fancy frame in a bright color, which matches one of the string colors, dresses up string art.

Ice Cream

Sometimes the simplest touches — a zigzagged cone and some rainbow sprinkles — make all the difference.

1 Trace the ice cream cone pattern, wrap the board, and insert the pins. Tear off the tracing paper.

2 Tie on the first color of string to the bottom pin. Zigzag the cone. Tie off.

3 In the second color, scribble or zigzag (see below) to fill in the ice cream. Then outline it.

4 Insert ball-head pins to look like rainbow sprinkles.

WHAT YOU NEED

- 1 small board
- 1 small background paper
- ice cream pattern (page 55)
- 1 small tracing paper
- 46 pins
- pin-pushing tool
- 2 colors of string
- ball-head pins

YOU'LL ALSO NEED
- tape
- pencil or fine-tip marker
- scissors
- glue

Mix it up: Instead of scribbling, zigzag side to side to fill in the top of the ice cream.

Zigzag Star

Zigzag five diamonds to form this bright star.

1 Trace the star pattern, wrap the board, and insert the pins. Tear off the tracing paper.

2 Tie on to an outer point of the star. Zigzag from that point to the center point, filling in a diamond-shaped section.

3 Moving clockwise, outline from the center point to the next outer point.

4 Repeat steps 2–3 until the star is filled in.

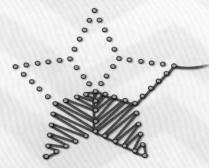

5 Outline all around the outer edge of the star.

It's okay that some edges have a double layer of outline, and others have a single layer.

WHAT YOU NEED

- 1 small board
- 1 small background paper
- zigzag star pattern (page 55)
- 1 small tracing paper
- 66 pins
- pin-pushing tool
- 1 color of string

YOU'LL ALSO NEED
- tape
- pencil or fine-tip marker
- scissors
- glue

Snail

Go slow with this snazzy snail and you'll be amazed by the result.

WHAT YOU NEED

- 1 large board
- 1 large background paper
- snail pattern (page 56)
- 1 large tracing paper
- 84 pins
- pin-pushing tool
- 2 colors of string
- 1 ball-head pin

YOU'LL ALSO NEED

- tape
- pencil or fine-tip marker
- scissors
- glue

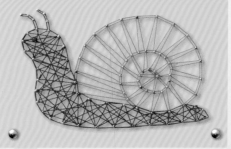

1 Trace the snail pattern, wrap the board, and insert the pins, except for the ball-head pin. Tear off the tracing paper.

2 Tie on the color for the snail shell where shown. Zigzag clockwise around in a circle, moving to the next pin each time. Pause where shown.

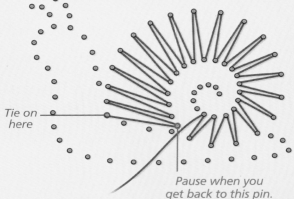

Tie on here

Pause when you get back to this pin.

3 Now the pattern changes. Continue to zigzag to the next pin when you go in toward the center, but skip every other pin when you go out. Pause where shown.

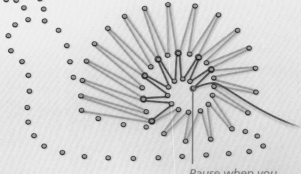

Pause when you get to this pin.

4 Now the pattern changes again. Continue to skip every other pin when you go out from the center. When you go in, return to the same pin each time, looping the string around it clockwise. Go out and in six times. Do not tie off.

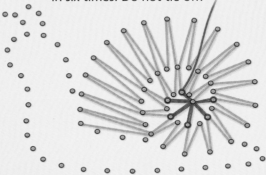

5 Double outline the coil as shown on page 21. Tie off.

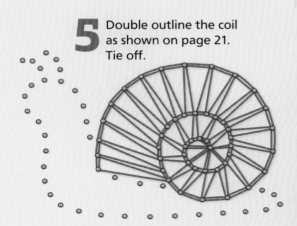

6 Tie on the second color of string to a pin on the snail's body. Scribble and outline the body and antennae. Insert a ball-head pin for an eye.

Patterns

Find the pattern for the project you want to do. Don't tear out the page. Simply line up tracing paper with the corners framing the pattern and trace the dots (see page 7). The dots show where you will put the pins.

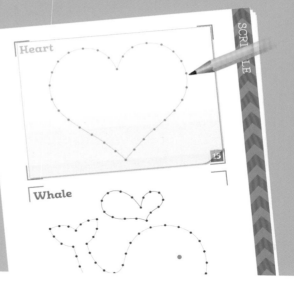

Scribble Star

17

Heart

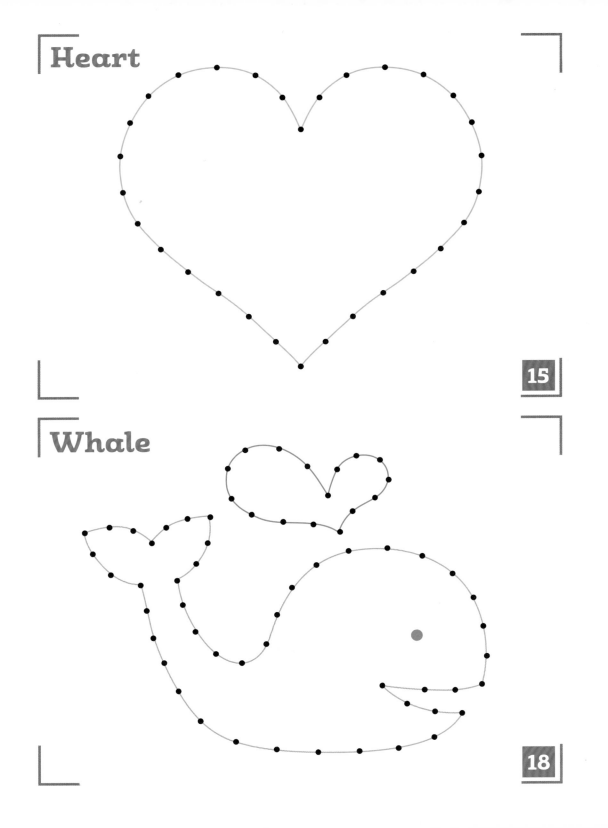

Whale

15

18

Cherries

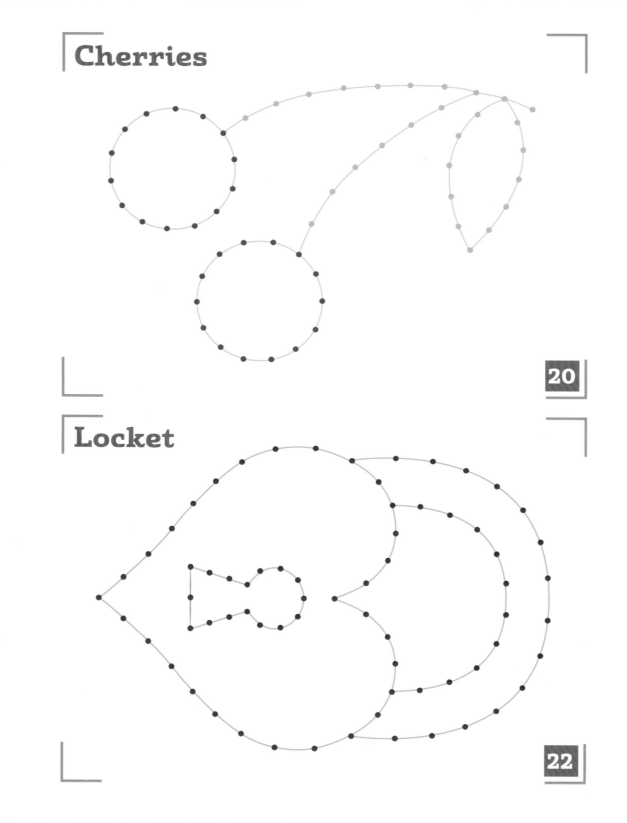

20

Locket

22

Glasses

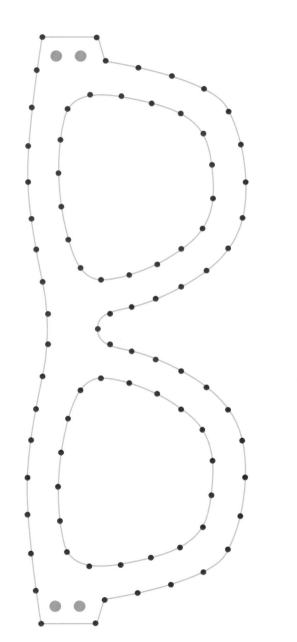

Love

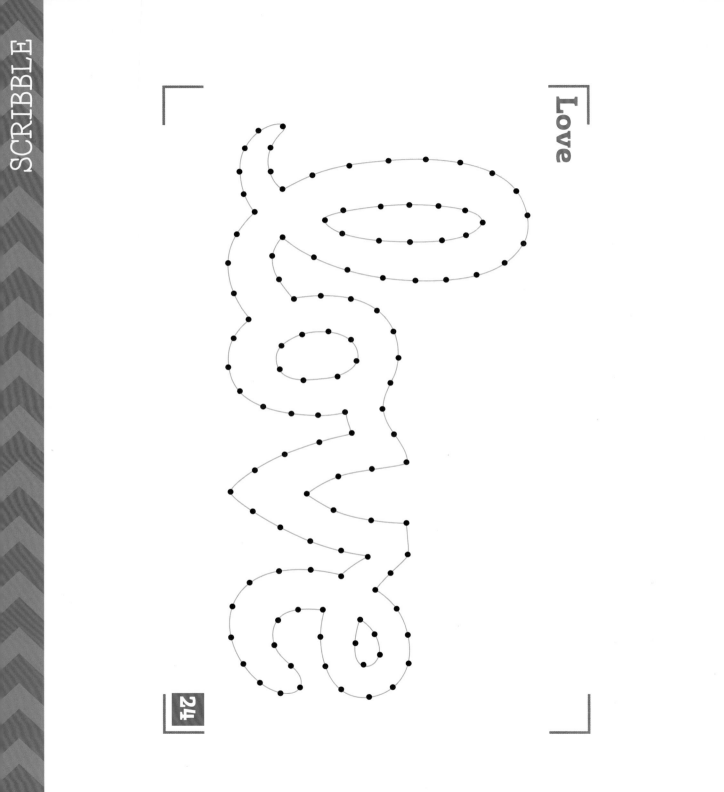

24

Butterfly

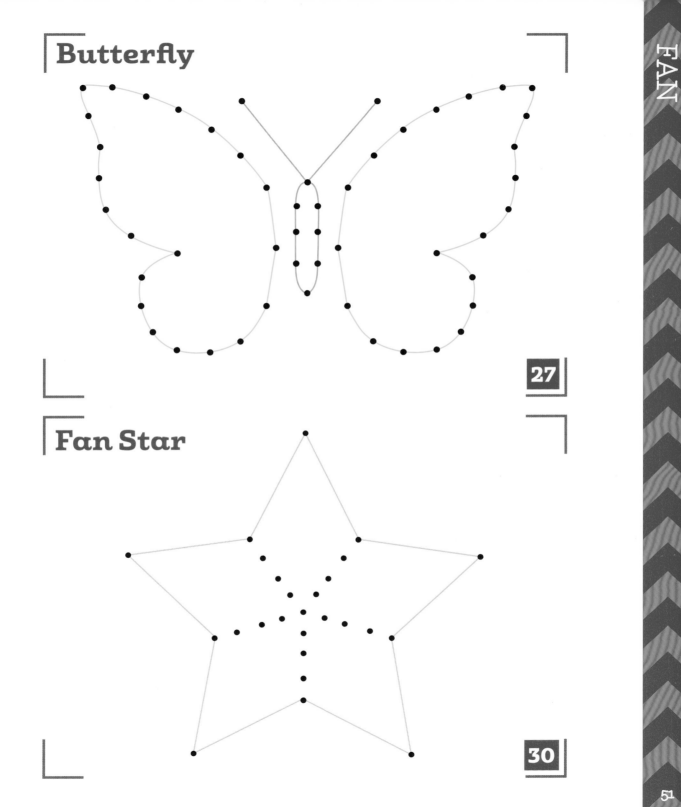

27

Fan Star

30

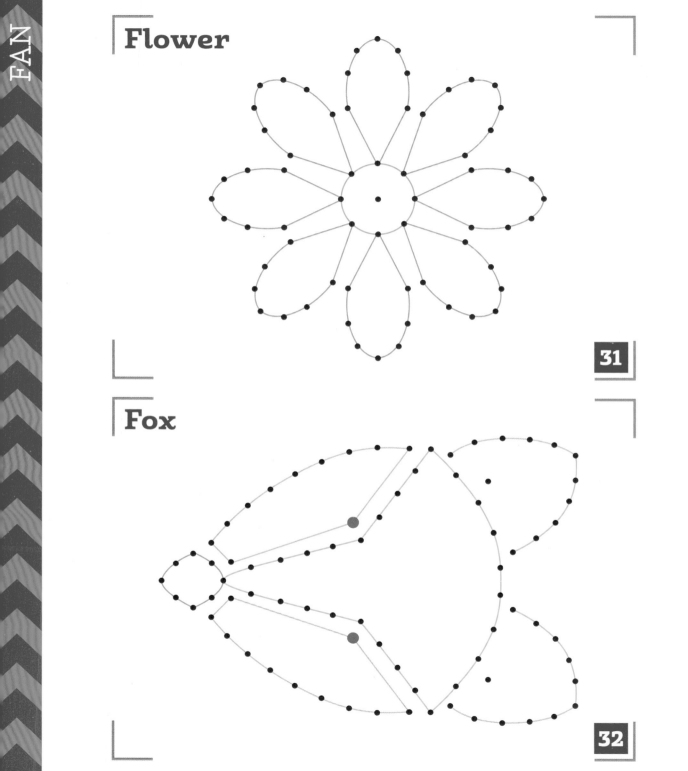

Flower

31

Fox

32

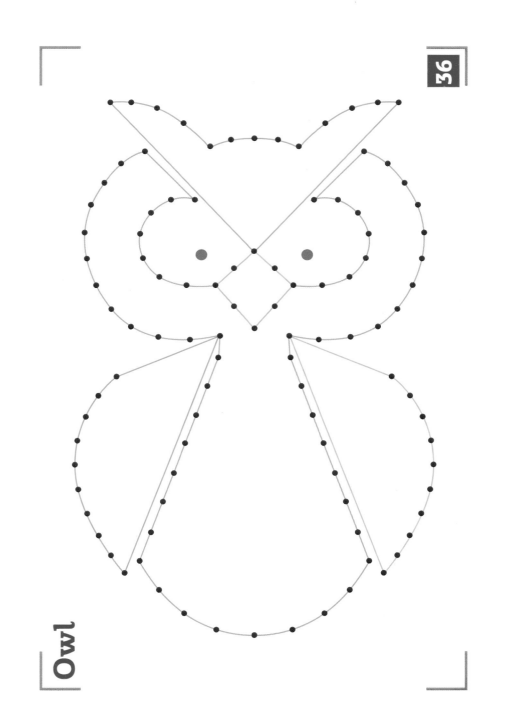

36

Owl

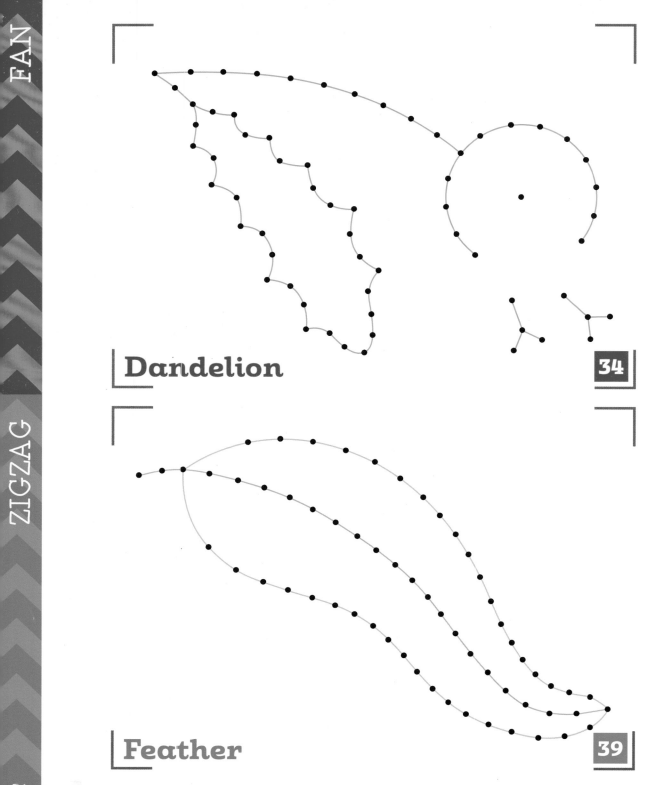

Dandelion

34

Feather

39